<u>Meet the author</u>

Nelson Paul Ragas Sr. is the creator of P'Knocks. He was born in New Orleans, Louisiana. However, he grew up in a small Louisiana town called Phoenix. Growing up, Nelson struggled with anger, self-confidence, and peer pressure. Throughout his childhood, Nelson often met other children who struggled with low self-esteem and behavior problems. They lacked motivation and many of them had little or no support. This was heartbreaking for Nelson because he too was dealing with some of the same issues. Later in his life, Nelson was inspired by his daughter Alissa's interest in animated characters. She enjoyed watching educational shows where the characters made learning fun and exciting.

One day, God gave Nelson a vision of a children's character that was both fun and educational. P'Knocks was born! Nelson created P'Knocks to educate and encourage children all over the world. He believes that children should have access to safe and supportive learning environments. P'Knocks encourages children to stay positive and never give up on their dreams. P'Knocks teaches children that doing the right thing and being a good person is cool.

Nelson Ragas works diligently, daily, to bring awareness of his P'Knocks character and to educate and empower children everywhere. He is blessed with a loving and supportive family and currently works as an officer for the Hammond, Louisiana Police Department.

To learn more about Nelson and his character P'Knocks visit www.pknocksrock.com

<u>**Dedication**</u>

This book is dedicated to my mother, Annabelle Thomas,

who is relaxing in Paradise with her Heavenly Father.

I can hear her voice encouraging me not to give up.

Despite your perseverance, be steadfast, immovable,

always abounding in the work of the Lord,

knowing that in the Lord,

your labor is not in vain.

I love you, mom!

Table of Contents

PKNOCKS A NEW KID THAT ROCKS

HOPE YOU ENJOY!

Meet P'Knocks

Years ago, Mr. and Mrs. Knocks had a handsome baby boy. They wanted him to grow up to be a young man who was kind and prosperous. Therefore, they decided to name him Prosperity. Through the years, as Prosperity was growing up, his mother began to call him P'Knocks for short. Once, the other children heard his nickname, they began to call him P'Knocks too. Thus, little Prosperity Knocks became known as P'Knocks to everyone around him.

Today, P'Knocks has grown into a happy young boy who is kind to everyone, including animals. P'Knocks has many friends and he is always a good friend to others. P'Knocks also loves learning new things and helping others solve problems. He is on a mission to help children all over the world to reach their goals through education and hard work.

P'Knocks believes that all children deserve love, attention and nurturing. They deserve to be safe and free to learn skills that will help them to grow into successful adults. P'Knocks works hard to encourage his friends to stay positive and develop good habits. P'Knocks knows that the kids who try the hardest are the coolest in town!

P. Knocks
KNOCK
P KNOCK

Learn with P'Knocks

Education is important to P'Knocks. P'Knocks knows that education is the key to knowledge, and knowledge is power. The world around us is full of things to learn. The more you learn, the more knowledge and wisdom you will have. School is a great place to obtain knowledge and learn new things.

P'Knocks loves to share the things that he learns with his classmates. P'Knocks teaches his friends that you should always respect others, including your teachers and other students. You should always be a good listener too.

When you are in class, you must listen to what your teacher is saying and follow directions. It is also important to work hard so that you can achieve your goals and become successful.

Learning is Important!

Learning is important

•Listen for instructions.
•Follow Directions!
•Work very hard.

I will learn every day, regardless of the situation.

Read with P'Knocks

P'Knocks loves to read. He is the president of his school's book club. On nice sunny days, P'Knocks likes to sit outside and read stories to his book club friends. P'Knocks tells his friends that reading is fun and helps to capture your imagination, tickle your funny bone and stimulate your creativity.

P'Knocks enjoys reading stories about peace, love, and success to his friends. He takes them on magical journeys that help them to calm down and relax after an adventurous day at school.

P'Knocks and his friends have fun in their book club. Book Clubs are a great way to learn more about books and the world around you. P'Knocks encourages children everywhere to join a book club and read more books.

READ! READ! READ!

<u>Reach Your Goals with P'Knocks</u>

P'Knocks is dedicated to helping his friends to pursue their dreams. He believes that it is important for children to learn about many different types of jobs. The world is full of jobs that people can do to help make a difference. P'Knocks teaches his friends that everyone's job is important.

P'Knocks asks his friends what they would like to be when they grow up. Everyone begins to tell P'Knocks what they want to be when they grow up. One friend says, "I want to be a Police Officer!" Police officer's jobs are to serve and protect the community. Another friend says, "I want to be a Firefighter!" Firefighters put out fires and rescue people in burning buildings.

A third friend tells P'Knocks, "I want to be a Doctor!" Doctors help people when they are sick to feel better. A fourth friend tells P'Knocks, "I want to be a Race Car Driver!" Race Car Drivers get to drive fast and race against other drivers. A fifth friend says, "I want to be a Pilot!" Pilots fly airplanes that take people and things to locations all over the world.

P'Knocks tells his friends that they can be whatever they want to be as long as they do their best!

What would you like to be when you grow up?

P Knocks
KNOCK
KNOCK
P
K
N

Get Fit With P'Knocks

Being healthy is important to P'Knocks. To be healthy, you must eat right and get exercise daily. P'Knocks tells his friends that it is very important to take care of your body because you only get one. He encourages his friends to eat healthy foods like fruits and vegetables daily.

 P'Knocks and his friends like to work out at the school gym. They work hard to make sure they stay fit and healthy. P'Knocks likes to educate his friends on how to stay healthy. P'Knocks reminds his friends that they should make sure they drink water daily because their bodies need water to survive.

P'Knocks tells his friends that it is also important to exercise daily.

Exercise! Exercise! Exercise!

NEWS ALERT!
PKNOCKS
A NEW KID THAT ROCKS
PKNOCKS
FITNESS
NEWS ALERT!
PKNOCKS
A NEW KID THAT ROCKS

P'Knocks Cares

P'Knocks wants to keep all of his friends safe. He is sad when one of his friends get hurt. P'Knocks is especially sad when one of his friends is bullied by another friend. P'Knocks encourages his friends to be kind to one another. P'Knocks wants all of his friends to work with him to help stop bullying. You can help P'Knocks put an end to bullying by learning and remembering the P'Knocks Pledge.

P'Knocks Anti-Bullying Pledge

I will not be a bully. I will not tell a Lie.

I will not hurt others. I will not make them cry.

I will keep my hands to myself and negative words too.

I will be respectful and kind in all that I do.

I will not judge others. I will not spread hate.

I will help save a life before It's too late.

I will not spread rumors. I will not prank or tease.

I will not be a part of this growing disease.

I will not ever criticize what I do not understand.

P Knocks
KNOCK KNOCK
P K

P'Knocks To The Rescue

P'Knocks and his friends are on a mission to help others. They are using their voices to take a stand and fight for what is right. P'Knocks and his friends have many causes they support and stand up for. P'Knocks feels sad when his friends are hurting. He does not want any of his friends to experience things like bullying or racism. P'Knocks travels all over the world, spreading messages of peace and love to his friends.

P'Knocks believes that everyone should be treated equally, and no one should be picked on just because of the color of their skin, where they live, or what they have. Cancer is another cause that P'Knocks is working hard to raise awareness. He and his friends encourage everyone to makes donations to help doctors find a cure for the disease.

P'Knocks wants his friends never to be afraid to stand up for something that they believe in. P'Knocks believes that everyone is a superhero, regardless of how big or small you are.

<u>*YOU* can make a difference.</u>

STOP
BULLYING
GET
ALONG
STOP
RACISM
ADOPT
A PET
KNOCK
KNOCK
P KNOCK
CURE
EDUCATION
IS
KEY TO
SUCCESS

Pray With P'Knocks

P'Knocks believes that prayer is very important. P'Knocks takes time to say his prayers every day. When P'Knocks pray, he says,

"Dear God, I pray the world will see good and follow you. I pray that you will help us to learn new things. Help us to be good people. Let my heart remember you in all that I do and help me not to be afraid, oh Lord! Help me to love everyone with my heart and in my actions.

"You can learn to pray with P'Knocks too! Get down on your knees, close your eyes, and repeat these words,

"Our Father, which art in Heaven, hallowed be your name. Your kingdom come, your will be done, on earth as it is in Heaven. Give us this day our daily bread, and forgive us our debts, as we also have forgiven our debtors. And lead us not into temptation but deliver us from evil. For thine is the kingdom, and the power, and the glory forever. In the Name of Jesus, AMEN!"

Be sure to say your prayers daily. Prayer gives us peace and helps us to stay connected to God.

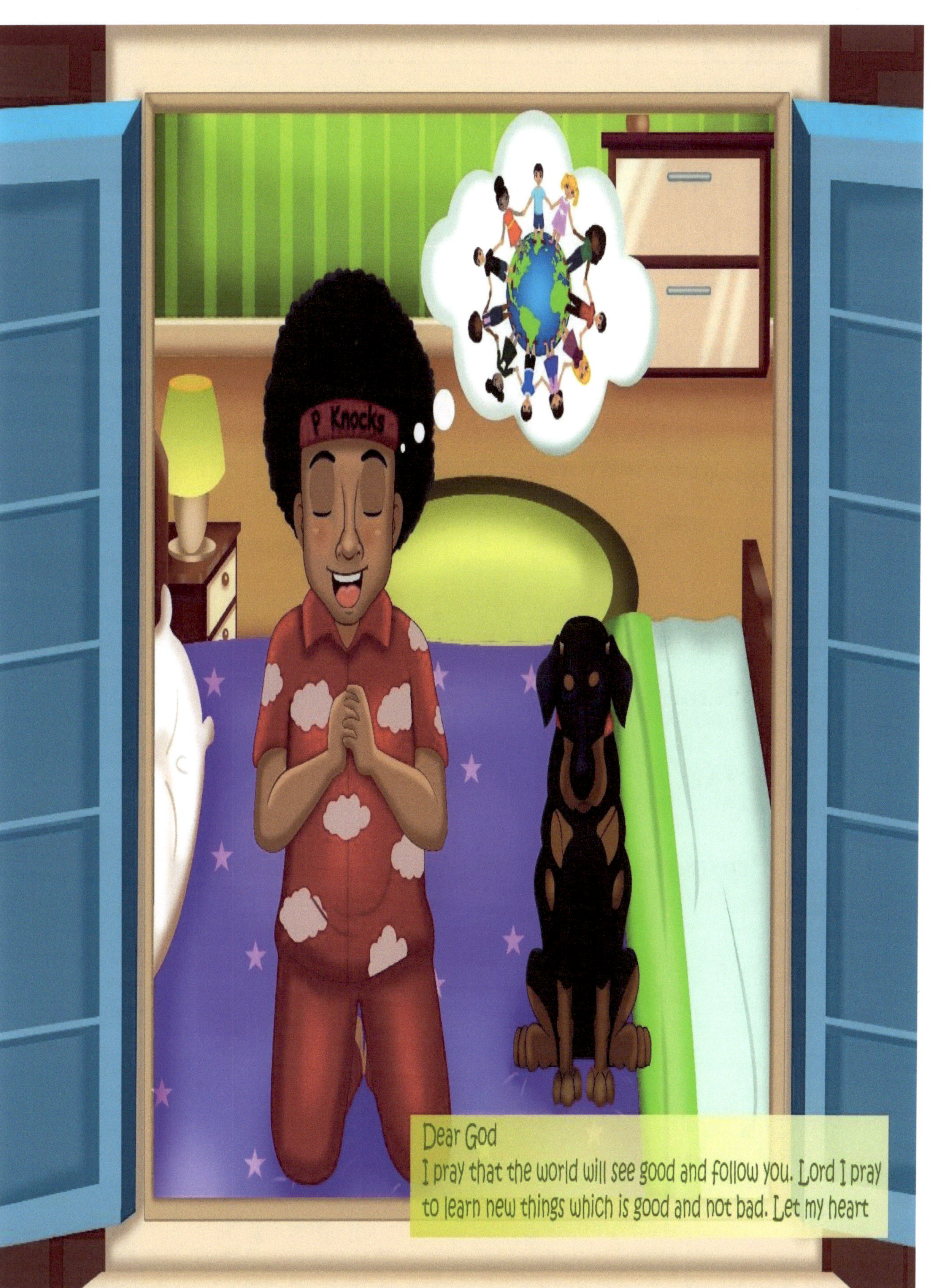
P Knocks
Dear God
I pray that the world will see good and follow you. Lord I pray
to learn new things which is good and not bad. Let my heart

Race To The Finish Line With P'Knocks

P'Knocks believes that everyone can be a winner if you work hard to reach your goals. P'Knocks is always cheering for his friends to win. He is happy when his friends reach their goals.

P'Knocks encourages his friends to have faith and believe that they can reach their goals. He reminds his friends that to win in life, they must stay away from bad behaviors and negative influences.

P'Knocks teaches his friends that everyone can be a winner if they work together.

Remember,

…Prosperity knocks when you do what rocks!

P knocks
P knocks
P knocks
P knocks
P knocks
Finish
Finish
Finish
Finish
Finish
Finish

P'Knocks wants you to remember to:

Pray often.

Ask questions.

Exercise daily.

Never be a bully.

Be nice to others.

Be kind to animals.

Read lots of books.

Always do your best.

Education is important.

Be respectful to others.

Always be a good listener.

Stay away from dream killers.

Never give up on your dreams.

Stand up for what you believe in

Eat healthy food and drink water.

Our mission is to equip children with the essential keys to grow, become positive role models, and strive for success in everything they do by leading, encouraging and educating.

~ Nelson Paul Ragas Sr.

P'Knocks encourage his friends to write daily. Find time throughout your day to write your dreams, goals, or inspirations to help encourage your success.

Pknocks A New Kid That Rocks

©Nelson Paul Ragas Sr, 2019-2020

My P'Knocks Personal Journal......

____

____

____

____

____

____

____

____

____

____.

<u>Follow us on social media:</u>

Facebook: Pknocks a new kid that rocks
Instagram: Pknocks
Twitter: joinpknocks

Remember Prosperity Knocks!
©Nelson Paul Ragas Sr, 2019-2020